Lord Mayors'
Portraits

DAME MARY DONALDSON
TO DAME FIONA WOOLF
1983–2013

Dame Mary Donaldson was the 656th Lord Mayor
of the City of London and the first woman elected
to the position in its more than 800-year history.
Dame Fiona Woolf was the 686th Lord Mayor and
only the second woman to hold the position.
By coincidence, portraits of the two women were
painted by the same artist, Richard Stone.

But where are the portraits of the other 684 Lord
Mayors in a role which began 825 years ago? If you
do happen to come across them in various livery
halls, the Mansion House, Guildhall Art Gallery or
other City institutions, there is virtually no
information about the portrait, the subject or the
artist.

Inspired by this fact, this book explores the tradition
of commissioning artists to paint portraits of Lord
Mayors, looks at the wide variety of resulting
portraits with comments from some of the artists
and talks about each Lord Mayor's time in office.

Going back before 1983 seemed a step too far, but commemorating Lord Mayors by creating a book of portraits beginning with the first female Lord Mayor Dame Mary and ending with Dame Fiona and focusing on the other Lord Mayors in between, seemed a distinct possibility.

And here is the result. A fascinating, informative, beautifully designed, high quality publication, written by people who know the City of London inside and out: Nicholas Woolf, Robert Woolf and Alexandra Epps.

"Portraiture is a hugely complicated process; you don't really know where a portrait is going to go. They all follow a format because they are official portraits but it is a two-way process and the real person is gradually revealed beneath the formal exterior."

DAME MARY DONALDSON GBE

The 650th Lord Mayor of London, Dame Mary was the first female Lord Mayor in a mayoralty stretching back nearly 800 years. In reaching this pinnacle, in 1966 she had been the first woman to be elected to the Court of Common Council, she went on to become the first female Alderman to be admitted to the Court and the first female Sheriff of the City. To her, gender was a complete irrelevance: at a Mansion House dinner describing her year she said, "Wherever I went, I found acceptance." Nevertheless, the title of the role in Lord Mayor and anyone referring to Dame Mary as the Lady Mayoress was asked to contribute £5 towards her Lord Mayor's Appeal, a box being kept on her desk for that purpose.

Dame Mary's natural theme for the year was It's People that Matter', an ethos she applied to her own life, having trained as a nurse during the Second World War. Her Lord Mayor's Appeal was on behalf of the NSPCC, for whom she campaigned tirelessly.

A feature of the Lord Mayor's Show is the swearing of the oath of allegiance to the Monarch at the Royal Courts of Justice. Accordingly, Dame Mary was presented to the Master of the Rolls, who happened to be her husband, Sir John Donaldson. This was a particularly pleasing event for them both as well as the Aldermen and others present, her credentials for the mayoralty being well known to Sir John!

Another light moment during her year included an incident at a livery company dinner when a paper shade protecting a candle from draughts caught fire. An over-enthusiastic member of staff threw a jug of water over it, and ruinously soaking Dame Mary. When it came to her turn to speak, she started by saying 'You've had the fire, then the flood, now you have the tempest."

Dame Mary was appointed a Justice of the Peace in 1960.

Dame Mary Donaldson died in October 2003 and her husband, elevated to the peerage in 1988, died in August 2005. He had taken the title of Lord Donaldson of Lymington.

Mother Ivory company Gardeners

To purchase a copy of the book, or for further information, please contact:

nicholas.woolf@btinternet.com
or visit www.artandlife.co.uk

Price £12.00 plus P&P

Lord Mayors' Portraits

DAME MARY DONALDSON
TO DAME FIONA WOOLF

1983–2013

Published 2015 by Art and Life (Publications)
39-41 North Road, London N7 9DP
www.artandlife.co.uk

Copyright © 2015 Nicholas Woolf, Robert Woolf and Alexandra Epps

British Library Cataloguing in Publication Data
A catalogue record for this book is available from the British Library

ISBN 978-0-9548122-3-2

Designed by Tim Epps
Photography by Julian Calder and Philip Traill
Edited by Emma Dawson

Printed in England by Impress Print Services
Hersham, Surrey KT12 3PU

CONTENTS

Left
Richard Stone painting the
portrait of Dame Fiona Woolf

Below
Discussing a sketch of the
proposed portrait at an early
sitting in the Mansion House

Below left
Unveiling the finished portrait
at The Worshipful Company
of Wax Chandlers

Photography: Julian Calder

FOREWORD

Notable people have traditionally had their portraits painted. No matter whether it is a circumstance of birth or a significant achievement, the great and the good have been celebrated with a portrait. Most are commissioned by the state, government, City corporations, civic institutions or, occasionally, by the sitter themselves. Typically, the portraits record the subject in a certain role, with all the trappings of wealth and status; in short, the embodiment of importance and a significant record to be passed into the annals of history.

The portrait painter's task is to not just paint the public face of the sitter but to capture something of the private self, something of a challenge when the sitter is bedecked with ceremonial robes to reflect their status. Selecting the robes of grand office, the background and the pose to communicate a message of authority has a long history in the tradition of British and European portraiture. In the hands of the great artists, the painted portrait can be lifted to a whole new level of pictorial quality and gravitas. One only has to think of Rembrandt's portraits of city burghers or the Court portraiture of Velázquez to see how portraits of officialdom can be elevated to masterpieces.

A high degree of finish often disguises the technical challenges necessary to bring the work about. The viewer is likely to give little thought to the palaver of arranging the sittings, often as not having had to contend with the subject's hectic diary. Artists are most likely to have to travel to the sitter, working away from the studio in unfamiliar surroundings, often grappling with unsatisfactory light sources and severe time restrictions, not to mention having to lug the studio necessities (easel, paint, canvas) to the sitter's residence or place of work. Many a subject will view the experience as a trial, others an occupational hazard but, every so often, some manage to enjoy it. For any artist, a new face presents a test of his or her abilities to record for posterity a person who has made a distinguished contribution to public life. I relish the challenge.

It has been said that portrait painting is a thing of the past and that the camera has killed it. However, looking back at the past thirty years of portraits of Lord Mayors, from Dame Mary Donaldson to Dame Fiona Woolf, I hope you will agree that the portraits add something to reflect the subject's achievements. A commissioned portrait is a complex phenomenon because it is the result of a unique and creative collaboration between artist and sitter. The distinguishing mark of a portrait is that it has a double function: it should be not only a convincing likeness of the sitter, capturing their personality and character, but also a pleasing object of art in composition, line and colour in its own right, in spite of all the ceremonial finery.

I hope that, along with my fellow portrait painters, we have achieved just that.

RICHARD STONE

INTRODUCTION

The inspiration for this book was both simple and startling. The Worshipful Company of Wax Chandlers had kindly commissioned a portrait to hang in the Company's Hall of my wife, Fiona, as Lord Mayor by the noted portrait artist Richard Stone. Fiona is a Liveryman of the Company. Richard was the obvious choice for the Wax Chandlers for two reasons: he is also a Liveryman of the Company but, incredibly, he had also painted the portrait of Dame Mary Donaldson, the Lord Mayor in 1983-84. Her portrait is known to everyone who has been Sheriff because it hangs in the Old Bailey, home to the Sheriffs. What a wonderful discovery that the portraits of the 656th Lord Mayor - and the first female Lord Mayor - and the 686th Lord Mayor - and second female Lord Mayor - have been painted by the same artist!

But where are the portraits of the other 684 Lord Mayors in a role which began 825 years ago? If you do happen to come across them in various livery halls, the Mansion House, Guildhall Art Gallery or other City institutions, there is virtually no information about the portrait, the subject or the artist. Going back before 1983 seemed a step too far, but commemorating Lord Mayors by creating a book of portraits beginning with the first female Lord Mayor and finishing with the second seemed a distinct possibility.

Tracking down the portraits and then the individual, or their families, proved challenging. Sir John Chalstrey's excellent book, The Aldermen of the City of London 1900-2010, provides biographical information of each person but we wanted to create more of a feel for both the personality and the memorable aspects of the mayoralty behind the portrait.

The traditions and history of the City, its livery companies and institutions, the pomp and ceremony, the philanthropy and good work are all reflected in various ways through Lord Mayors' portraits, a custom that records their achievements, endeavour and service.

Having conceived the idea for this book once Fiona's mayoralty had begun, I was not able in my role as The Lord Mayor's Consort to carry out such an ambitious project on my own. I was delighted, therefore, to have the assistance of two fellow authors (credited on the inside front cover): my brother Robert Woolf and Alexandra Epps, both qualified City of London Guides.

It has not been easy to find some of the portraits and indeed four of the 31 Lord Mayors in this period do not have mayoral portraits. For them we have resorted to 'official' photographic images as we did not wish to have an incomplete collection. Overall, it has been a fascinating and very rewarding challenge. We have learned a great deal and have been down some interesting paths in researching and pursuing material, all of which is hopefully reflected in this book. We are very grateful to the Lord Mayors and their families for willingly collaborating in this project, as well as various livery companies, photographers (particularly Julian Calder), the City of London Corporation and Tim Epps, who brought it all together, designing and masterminding the final product.

I very much hope that the various elements of the Civic City, including the 110 livery companies, as well as the art and portrait world, will find the book both interesting and informative.

NICHOLAS WOOLF
The Lord Mayor's Consort 2013-14

The Portraits

DAME MARY DONALDSON GBE

The 656th Lord Mayor of London, Dame Mary was the first female Lord Mayor in a mayoralty stretching back nearly 800 years. In reaching this pinnacle, in 1966 she had been the first woman to be elected to the Court of Common Council. She went on to become the first female Alderman to be admitted to the Court and the first female Sheriff of the City. To her, gender was a complete irrelevance - at a Mansion House dinner describing her year she said, "Wherever I went, I found acceptance." Nevertheless, the title of the role is Lord Mayor and anyone referring to Dame Mary as the Lady Mayoress was asked to contribute £5 towards her Lord Mayor's Appeal, a box being kept on her desk for that purpose.

Dame Mary's mayoral theme for the year was 'It's People that Matter', an ethos she applied to her own life, having trained as a nurse during the Second World War. Her Lord Mayor's Appeal was on behalf of the NSPCC, for whom she campaigned tirelessly.

A feature of the Lord Mayor's Show is the swearing of the oath of allegiance to the Monarch at the Royal Courts of Justice. Accordingly, Dame Mary was presented to the Master of the Rolls, who happened to be her husband, Sir John Donaldson. This was a particularly pleasing event for them both as well as the Aldermen and others present, her credentials for the mayoralty being well known to Sir John!

Another light moment during her year included an incident at a livery company dinner when a paper shade protecting a candle from draughts caught fire. An over-enthusiastic member of staff threw a jug of water over it, unfortunately soaking Dame Mary. When it came to her turn to speak, she started by saying: "You've had the fire, then the flood, now you have the tempest."

Dame Mary was appointed a Justice of the Peace in 1960.

Dame Mary Donaldson died in October 2003 and her husband, elevated to the peerage in 1988, died in August 2005. He had taken the title of Lord Donaldson of Lymington.

Mother livery company Gardeners.

Richard Stone

1985

Oil on canvas

127 x 102cms (50 x 40ins)

Old Bailey

"*I felt honoured to be asked to paint Dame Mary. I was given free rein in how to approach the commission. Dame Mary is shown seated in the Mansion House on an early 19th century chair from a set known traditionally as the 'Nile Suite', linking them to the battles of Lord Nelson, specifically to the 1798 Battle of the Nile.*"
RICHARD STONE
(*See also Sir Allan Davis and Dame Fiona Woolf*)

SIR ALAN TRAILL GBE

Sir Alan's theme for his mayoral year was 'Living with Harmony' and reflected both his passion for music and his concerns over social discord in Britain at the time. His mayoralty commenced during the 1984-85 nationwide coal miners' strike.

His Lord Mayor's Appeal supported the St Paul's Choir School Foundation which he had established and raised substantial funds on their behalf. His Appeal also supported Treloar School and College, a special needs school set up in 1907 by Sir William Treloar, the then Lord Mayor. Treloar's continues to occupy a special place in the hearts of the City livery companies. The school and college have become one of the country's leading providers of education, care and independence training for disabled young people and former pupils were contestants in the 2012 Paralympic Games in London. The Traill Centre was opened by Prince Charles in 1987 and today houses a business enterprise and other college services.

Sir Alan started his City business career in insurance in 1956 and founded his own insurance brokerage firm in 1973.

Personal musical highlights of his mayoralty included conducting the overture to The Marriage of Figaro at the Barbican Arts Centre and conducting the massed bands at the Royal Tournament playing Elgar's Pomp & Circumstance March No 1.

A unique spectacle at his Lord Mayor's Show was that of Sir Alan's wife, Sarah, riding a horse side-saddle, looking most distinguished. By so doing, she reinstated the presence of The Lady Mayoress in The Lord Mayor's Show for the first time since the reign of Queen Victoria.

Mother livery company Cutlers (Master 1979).
Also: Master Musician (2000).

Andrew Festing

1995

Oil on canvas

125 x 99cms (49 x 39ins)

Cutlers' Hall

"Portraiture is a hugely complicated process; you don't really know where a portrait is going to go. They all follow a format because they are official portraits but it is a two-way process and the real person is gradually revealed beneath the formal exterior."
ANDREW FESTING
(See also Sir Alexander Michael Graham, Lord Levene and Nick Anstee)

SIR ALLAN DAVIS GBE

Sir Allan's theme for the year was 'Service with a Smile' and this very much typified the approach of Sir Allan and the Lady Mayoress. During his mayoralty, Sir Allan managed to reflect and share his faith, his many charitable interests and his professional commitment to the City of London. With the help of the Evening Standard newspaper a search was made for the Londoner that epitomised the theme with an assessment panel that included Tommy Steele, Miss UK and Sir Peter Parker, Chairman of British Rail. His Lord Mayor's Appeal raised funds principally for the British Foundation for Age Research.

Sir Allan qualified as a chartered accountant with Dunn Wylie in 1949 and he remained with the firm, rising to senior partner. When the firm merged in 1976 with Armitage and Norton, he became senior partner from 1979 until his retirement in 1986.

Among the notable overseas visits performing his mayoral duties were Sir Allan's ten days in May 1986 when he journeyed to Luxembourg, then New York and Washington. In Washington he marked the tenth anniversary of Concorde's commercial service, before travelling to Oslo. In August he travelled to Trinidad and Tobago where he had been stationed with the Fleet Air Arm during the Second World War.

With all his visits Sir Allan brought to his year a relaxed style while energetically promoting the City, commerce and entrepreneurial activity at a time of great national change. The City was preparing for the coming of de-regulation and the nation was enthused by the creation of the Channel Tunnel project.

Sir Allan was always keen to involve his family in his mayoral year. A Whitbread dray carried all his family in the Lord Mayor's Show and they have many happy memories of attending gatherings in the Mansion House.

Sir Allan Davis died in 1994.

Mother livery company Painter-Stainers.

Richard Stone

1986

Oil on canvas

91 x 71 cms (36 x 28ins)

Painters' Hall

Reproduced by kind permission of The Worshipful Company of Painter-Stainers, London

SIR DAVID ROWE-HAM GBE

Sir David adopted as his Lord Mayor's Appeal the Prince of Wales's Youth Business Trust which exists to assist young unemployed people in setting up their own business. His mayoralty was also notable for the inauguration of the Lord Mayor's Awards for Business Involvement in the Community, known as the Dragon Awards. Subsequent Lord Mayors have continued to oversee the Dragon Awards which have become a prominent scheme celebrating Community Engagement programmes. The Awards form part of the City of London Corporation's commitment to engaging business and public offices in the regeneration of local communities recognising that the City will not prosper in isolation. An annual Awards dinner is hosted by the Lord Mayor at the Mansion House.

Sir David's theme for the year was 'The City of London Working for Britain' which reflected his wide business experience in accountancy and stock-broking and as a board director of a number of quoted and private companies.

At the beginning of his mayoralty, Sir David unveiled a plaque beside Queenhithe dock on the River Thames to mark the 1100th anniversary of the resettlement by King Alfred in the year 886 of the City of London. Queenhithe is no longer used as a dock and the City is focused on its world-wide role in financial and related services. In October 1986 deregulation of financial markets took place - known as the 'Big Bang' - and Sir David travelled extensively during the year to promote the benefits of the City of London and the UK's financial services industry.

Of many highlights, Sir David was honoured to receive the Queen in the City on the occasion of Her Majesty granting new colours to the Honourable Artillery Company, the oldest regiment in the British Army, during their 450th anniversary year.

Mother livery company Wheelwrights.
Also: Master Chartered Accountant (1985-86).

Margaret Palmer

1987

Oil on canvas

102 x 76cms (40 x 30ins)

In private ownership

"When painting an official portrait it is important to include all of the finery and pomp of the 'uniform'. The ermine, hat, gloves and mayoral chair all enhance the formality of the pose and role of Lord Mayor. Capturing in paint the details of the fine lace and velvet are always a delight."
MARGARET PALMER

SIR GREVILLE SPRATT GBE TD DL

Sir Greville's mayoral theme was 'Make an Extra Effort for Britain' and he led by example. His Lord Mayor's Appeal supported three charities for the benefit of children: Action Research for the Crippled Child (now known as Action Medical Research), Great Ormond Street Children's Hospital and the Treloar Trust.

Sir Greville was an underwriting member of Lloyd's of London and later in his career he joined his father-in-law's electrical distributor business, J & N Wade, becoming managing director.

As Lord Mayor, Sir Greville had the distinction in June 1988 of receiving President Reagan of the United States at a luncheon in Guildhall which was also attended by Prime Minister Margaret Thatcher. President Reagan was returning to America from a successful summit meeting in Moscow with President Gorbachev at which a treaty on arms reduction had been ratified and talks had taken place on reducing the numbers of strategic missiles. The tone of President Reagan's speech at Guildhall was serious and very moving when he spoke of free nations, their love of freedom and yearnings for peace. Yet the speech also contained humorous touches when, for example, he referred to the 15th century Guildhall as being somewhat older than himself.

Prior to his mayoralty, Sir Greville had a successful military career, commanding the Honourable Artillery Company, becoming Regimental Colonel and ADC to Her Majesty the Queen. He was therefore delighted to join the Regiment in Boston to attend the celebration in mid-1988 of the 350th anniversary of the Ancient and Honourable Artillery Company of Massachusetts.

After his mayoralty had ended, an athletics stadium was opened and named after Sir Greville at Charterhouse School where he had been a pupil and had excelled at athletics. The School was founded in 1611 on the site of a Carthusian Monastery at Smithfield outside London's City wall.

Sir Greville Spratt died in December 2012. Lady Spratt died in 2002.

Mother livery company Ironmongers (Master 1995-96).

Gareth Hawker

1989

Oil on canvas

102 x 71cms (40 x 28ins)

Ironmongers' Hall

"*I prefer to paint people standing as you get a better bearing, particularly when the subject holds a high rank. It is the relationship between the head, neck and shoulders - getting the best of the person, seeing their best side. I enjoyed the challenge of realistically portraying the fine details of the chain of office, the jewel and the delicate lace of the jabot.*"
GARETH HAWKER

SIR CHRISTOPHER COLLETT GBE

Sir Christopher's mayoral year was a special one during which the City celebrated the 800th year of the mayoralty with the objectives to involve people, be educational, interest the younger generation, benefit charities, provide enjoyment, give a sense of history and establish permanent mementos. During the year, many events, exhibitions (including both the first livery companies exhibition and 'Dick Whittington: the man and the myth' in Guildhall) and concerts were held, the Cutty Sark Tall Ships race started from London bound for Hamburg, the 800th year Anniversary Scholarships were established at City schools and some thirty charities benefited from fundraising.

Using the anniversary to launch the Appeal, The Lord Mayor's 800th Anniversary Awards Trust aimed to help young people expand their horizons with purposeful travel and built on the mayoral theme of 'People Count'. Over the years the Trust has been a marked success.

Sir Christopher started his accountancy career with Cassleton Elliott & Co in 1954. Through a series of mergers he ultimately became a senior partner in Ernst & Young.

His grandfather and his uncle both served as Lord Mayor of London and his father was a Common Councilman. Another uncle was Chief Commoner.

In April 1989, Sir Christopher received President Gorbachev at Guildhall where the President made his 'perestroika' speech. Prime Minister Margaret Thatcher responded, referring to rights and freedoms that were forged in the City of London. In May, in a speech following the presentation to her of the Honorary Freedom of the City of London the Prime Minister thanked all present and made her eloquent statement of the contribution of the City to the UK and her suggestion that if Westminster is the mother of parliaments, then the City must be the grandmother of parliaments.

Of particular interest within the 'Square Mile', Sir Christopher hosted a Guildhall reception on the occasion of the 150th anniversary of the formation of the City Police Force. After his mayoralty, Sir Christopher became chairman of the Temple Bar Trust which achieved its aim of returning Wren's Temple Bar gateway to the City. Now refurbished, this stands at Paternoster Square next to St Paul's Cathedral.

Sir Christopher Collett died in December 2012.

Mother livery company Glovers (Master 1981-82).

Jane Allison

1989

Oil on canvas

76 x 61cms (30 x 24ins)

In private ownership

"I like to paint people with interesting clothes and interesting lives. I wanted to create a historical object to stand the test of time. Portraits are a two-way process between sitter and artist - a joint enterprise. I particularly enjoyed painting the chain of office which I built up with a series of glazes and many layers of paint."
JANE ALLISON

ALLISON 1989

SIR HUGH BIDWELL GBE

Sir Hugh Bidwell was installed as the 662nd Lord Mayor 800 years after the first Mayor, Henry Fitz-Ailwin, took office in 1189.

For the Lord Mayor's Appeal, Sir Hugh and his wife Jenny, the Lady Mayoress, chose to work together rather than by the then convention of having separate charities. Their combined efforts were successful in fundraising for Age Concern, Action on Addiction and Crisis for the Homeless.

In his memoir, Sir Hugh wrote that as Lord Mayor he went out of his way to be as inclusive as possible, determined not to be seduced by the grandeur and prestige of his office. As an example, on Christmas Day he visited City police stations to talk to the officers on duty. This reflected his approach to treat everyone with the same respect.

Sir Hugh's successful business career in the food industry enabled him to bring a strong sense of marketing to the City and he focused on measures to boost the City's profile. He was chairman of Pearce Duff for 15 years until 1984 when it was sold to Gill and Duffus. He continued to serve the food industry in international roles and as president of the British Food Export Council.

In his speech at his Lord Mayor's Banquet he emphasised the need for improvements to London's transport system and the point was recognised by Prime Minister Margaret Thatcher. A Bill was introduced into Parliament in 1991 promoting 'Crossrail' although it took time for the project to become a reality. As regards overseas trade, Britain benefitted from his deep under-standing of commerce and as Lord Mayor he felt he was able to influence foreign governments in their dealings with British companies.

Unusually in the 800-year history of the mayoralty, Sir Hugh experienced an earth tremor while at a civic luncheon in Liverpool.

Lady Bidwell died in 2001. In 2003, Sir Hugh married Mrs Priscilla Pode (née Hunter). Sir Hugh Bidwell died in December 2013.

Mother livery company Grocers (Master 1984-85).

Anna Partridge

1990

Watercolour with gold leaf on ivorine

Portrait miniature
7 x 6cms (2.75 x 2.3ins)

In private ownership

*Photograph of painting:
Michael Chevis*

SIR ALEXANDER MICHAEL GRAHAM GBE

The theme of Sir Alexander's mayoralty was 'Moving Ahead' as he focused his efforts on the City and UK as a whole, taking advantage of business opportunities offered by the European Single Market. There was at the time anxiety that Frankfurt would become a major competitor to the City of London and it was pleasing that during his mayoral year the European Bank for Reconstruction and Development opened for business with its headquarters in the City.

After leaving St Paul's School, Sir Alexander joined the insurance brokerage firm of Frizzell & Partners. He became group managing director in 1973 and deputy chairman in 1990, retiring from the firm in 1993.

As Lord Mayor, Sir Alexander was the first senior non-political figure to visit Argentina after diplomatic relations between Britain and Argentina were re-established following the Falklands conflict. During his mayoral visit to South America he visited Chile to join celebrations for the 450th anniversary of the founding of Santiago. While there, he was entertained by President Aylwin, a distant descendent of the first Mayor of London in 1189. Unlike today, when the office is held for one year, Henry Fitz-Ailwin held office from 1189 until his death in 1212. The title of 'Lord Mayor' only came into use in the 14th century.

Sir Alexander recalled that by the end of his mayoral year he had received 105 ties. One gift in particular required a diplomatic response from the Lord Mayor when visiting Mumbai (then Bombay). He had addressed the Bombay Chamber of Commerce and Industry (BCCI) and at the end of his address was presented with a tie with the initials BCCI on it. Unfortunately, a bank whose name was abbreviated to BCCI collapsed at that time, causing considerable loss to many individuals, particularly in the Middle East and India. Sir Alexander thanked the Chamber of Commerce for their kind gift, venturing to remark that, whilst their kindness was appreciated, in view of the very considerable bad feelings surrounding the bank's collapse, he doubted he would be able to wear it in the near future. His humorous touch was well received by the audience.

Mother livery company Mercers (Master 1983-84).

Andrew Festing

1993

Oil on canvas

102 x 79cms (40 x 32ins)

Mercers' Hall

Photograph of painting:
Louis Sinclair

SIR BRIAN JENKINS GBE

Sir Brian was Lord Mayor in the year the European Single Market was created and his theme for the year, 'The City Serving Europe', reflected the challenge to the City of London from this event. Accordingly, he made numerous trips throughout Europe to emphasise the business strengths of the City.

Recognising that the UK economy was still in recession, Sir Brian wanted his Lord Mayor's Appeal to take a different approach from just seeking funds. He therefore established, through Community Service Volunteers, a programme to improve connections between universities and schools. The Appeal was called 'Learning Together' and by the fifth year some 10,000 undergraduate students were involved in the programme in 3,000 schools.

Sir Brian had a distinguished career as a chartered accountant during which he served as president of the Institute of Chartered Accountants in England and Wales from 1985-86. He qualified with Cooper Brothers as the firm was then known in 1963. A partner in the firm from 1969, he became a member of its UK executive committee. Sir Brian left the firm in 1995 and was appointed as chairman of the Woolwich Building Society (subsequently Woolwich plc) and later became deputy chairman of Barclays Bank.

Sir Brian and the City had the difficult task of dealing with the bombing of the Baltic Exchange. This occurred on the evening of Friday 10 April 1992 and Sir Brian led City efforts to ensure that the Exchange was running again by the following Tuesday. On 16 September 1992, the UK left the Exchange Rate Mechanism, an event which became known as 'Black Wednesday'. Sir Brian was travelling in Scandinavia at the time, and was able to reassure those countries that they could continue to rely upon London as their financial trading partner.

As a member of the Honourable Artillery Company, Sir Brian was invited to take part in the 'final shoot' of the Army's 25-pounder gun to celebrate its retirement after 50 years. By virtue of a misfire, his was the last to be fired operationally in the British Army.

Mother livery company Chartered Accountants (Master 1990-91).
Also: Master Information Technologist (1994-95) and Master Merchant Taylor (1999-2000).

Jane Bond

1996

Oil on canvas

53 x 45cms (21 x 18ins)

Chartered Accountants' Hall

"The painting was to be smaller than usual, determined by its location in the Chartered Accountants' Hall. I still wanted Sir Brian to be life size and so I concentrated on the head and shoulders. I love painting fabrics and fine detail and enjoyed painting the jabot, chain and jewel, I also included his coat of arms painted as if an embroidered tapestry."
JANE BOND
(See also Sir David Wootton)

SIR FRANCIS McWILLIAMS GBE

The theme of Sir Francis's mayoralty was 'The City and Industry in Partnership' and he sought to increase the traditional involvement of the livery companies in education and training in their trades or professions. Sir Francis formed the 'Adoption of Schools Working Party' from which, in 2003, the Livery Schools Link arose. Today the Link acts as a focal point through which the education community may make contact with livery companies. The Register of Engineers for Disaster Relief (RedR) and a foundation for manufacturing and industry both benefitted from his mayoral appeal.

Sir Francis had lived in Malaysia for some 23 years, engaged in a variety of construction projects, and on his return to the UK he studied law, being called to the Bar in Lincoln's Inn in 1978. With this background, Sir Francis sat on the Guildhall Yard East Committee which dealt with the redevelopment of the Guildhall Art Gallery. Following the excavations uncovering a 12th century chapel and the wonderful discovery of remains of the Roman amphitheatre, major changes to the gallery design were necessary and these were carried out by Richard Gilbert Scott whose father Sir Giles was the architect commissioned to restore Guildhall in the 1950s.

Sir Francis's home for much of his mayoral year was in medieval Ironmonger Lane until the completion of a major refurbishment of the Mansion House, the Lord Mayor's official residence.

On a mayoral visit to Malaysia to promote British engineering and construction companies, Sir Francis was able to use his fluency in the Malay language to good effect. He repeated this by opening his speech in Malay at a banquet to mark the state visit to the City of the King of Malaysia, His Majesty Yang Di-Pertuan Agong.

Mother livery company Loriners (Master 1995-96).
Also: Master Arbitrator (1985-86) and Master Engineer (1990-91).

Artist unknown

1993

Oil on canvas

130 x 106cms (51 x 41ins)

Plaisterers' Hall

SIR PAUL NEWALL TD DL

Sir Paul's mayoral theme was 'The International City - the World is our Market' which reflected his business experience in New York and London. His recognition of the UK's strong financial services, and high quality 'back office' support, helped to attract inward investment and create jobs. Sir Paul's discussions with Samsung's chairman assisted in a plant being set up in north east England.

His Lord Mayor's Appeal raised funds for the restoration of St Paul's Cathedral and he was a trustee of the Endowment Trust for several years after his mayoralty. The restoration, completed in 2011, has resulted in external facades of the Cathedral probably looking better than at any time since it was completed some 300 years ago.

Sir Paul began his business career with stockbrokers Cazenove, working on the floor of the Stock Exchange. Then, after working for a time in the New York Stock Exchange, he returned to London to become an institutional broker advising companies on American investment. In the 1990s he became a director and adviser to Lehman Brothers.

At a tense time in Middle East affairs, his visit to Kuwait and a conversation with the Emir that Kuwait could count on British support brought thanks from the Foreign Secretary and a unique mayoral visit to a Royal naval frigate patrolling in the Persian Gulf.

Sir Paul was a champion fencer in his youth and during his mayoral visit to Budapest he fenced against the current Hungarian Olympic sabre champion. On another overseas visit he was able to offer suggestions on how to reduce trouble from rats by quoting the experience of the fabled Dick Whittington, who in reality was Richard Whittington, Lord Mayor of London and City benefactor.

Mother livery company Bakers (Master 1990-91).
Also: Founder Master International Bankers (2001-02).

Carlos Sancha

1994

Oil on canvas

152 x 117cms (60 x 46ins)

Bakers' Hall

The painting shows Sir Paul standing on the steps of the Mansion House with St Paul's Cathedral beyond. This view is no longer available as buildings now obscure the view. Mr Sancha took advantage of a temporary redevelopment opportunity and a little artistic licence but, nevertheless, provided an interesting variation on a traditional theme.

SIR CHRISTOPHER WALFORD

Sir Christopher chose the British Heart Foundation as the focus of his charitable appeal, primarily because Anne, his Lady Mayoress, had for some years suffered from a comparatively rare heart condition. The Appeal enjoyed a successful outcome, with significant support from City institutions and individual donors. A highlight of the Appeal was the piano recital given at The Queen's House, Greenwich by Fanny Waterman (co-founder of the Leeds International Piano Competition) and the then Lord Chief Justice, Peter Taylor.

Linked with this charitable appeal was Sir Christopher's mayoral theme, 'The City - the Heart of the Nation', intended to proclaim both the unequalled record of the City of London as a highly successful international financial centre and its ongoing role as a major provider of jobs and overseas earnings for the nation as a whole. In furtherance of his theme, Sir Christopher visited virtually all the principal business centres in the UK outside London to address in particular the important links between the City and British industry.

Sir Christopher was the first solicitor to have been elected Lord Mayor since Sir Cullum Welch in 1956. He was also the only Lord Mayor in comparatively recent times to have been Mayor of a London Borough, having been Mayor of the Royal Borough of Kensington and Chelsea in 1979.

Among the memorable events that occurred during Sir Christopher's mayoralty was the magnificent banquet given by the Corporation in Guildhall to commemorate the 50th anniversary of VE Day, attended by Her Majesty the Queen, HRH the Duke of Edinburgh and many other members of the Royal Family, together with 58 other state or government leaders.

Other notable events were the receptions held at Guildhall to mark the centenary of the Commercial Court, seen worldwide as the pre-eminent specialist commercial court for international dispute resolution, and the 780th anniversary of the sealing of Magna Carta, for which a reception was held at Guildhall. The City's own 1297 Magna Carta includes Edward I's seal and was displayed in the 2014 Lord Mayor's Show as a precursor to the 800th anniversary celebrations to be held in 2015.

Lady Walford died in 2004. In 2009 Sir Christopher married Denise Hudson.

Mother livery company Makers of Playing Cards (Master 1987-88).
Also: Master Solicitor (1993-94).

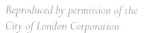

Reproduced by permission of the City of London Corporation

SIR JOHN CHALSTREY

Sir John was the first surgeon to hold the office of Lord Mayor although in 1550, Sir John Ayliffe, surgeon to King Henry VIII, was elected to the Court of Aldermen. He died before he was able to achieve the office of Lord Mayor.

Sir John Chalstrey's mayoral theme was 'Good Health to the City and the Nation'. This reflected his belief in the huge benefits of having a national policy that encourages a healthy lifestyle. He combined this message with the promotion of British medicine and medical products.

His Mayoral Appeal supported St John Ambulance of which he was Surgeon-in-Chief and remained so until 1999. The Order of St John has been an order of chivalry since the Crusades and, although abolished during the Reformation in England, was revived in 1888. Today, the Order of St John is known internationally for its first aid and ambulance services and the St John of Jerusalem Eye Hospital.

Sir John has had a distinguished career as a surgeon. In 1975, he established the first fibre-optic endoscopy unit in the independent healthcare sector. On retirement from the NHS in 1996, he was appointed Emeritus Surgeon to St Bartholomew's and the Royal London hospitals. From 1998-2008 he was chairman of their fundraising committee and a trustee of its charitable foundation.

Sir John has strong memories of President Nelson Mandela's State Visit to the UK in 1996. Her Majesty the Queen, concerned for President Mandela's health, had indicated that the Mayoral Banquet at the Mansion House should not finish late. However, as The Lord Mayor and guests proceeded out of the Egyptian Hall after the Banquet, Nelson Mandela shook hands and spoke with everyone on his path to the front door. A large crowd that had assembled outside the Mansion House cheered as the President emerged and he went forward to chat with many of them. It was thus quite late before his car departed for Buckingham Palace. In view of the Queen's admonition of the previous day, Sir John's sleep was disturbed by dreams of the Monarch anxiously waiting while the Lord Mayor, escorted by Yeoman Warders, was taken to the Tower of London!

Mother livery company Apothecaries (Master 1994-95). Also: Master Barber (1998-99).

June Mendoza

1996

Oil on canvas

91 x 71cms (36 x 28ins)

Apothecaries' Hall

"I included the interior of the Mansion House in the background to capture the aura and atmosphere of the role of Lord Mayor; to provide a narrative without taking away from the personality of the sitter - the man is there before the robes are added."
JUNE MENDOZA
(See also Sir David Brewer)

SIR ROGER CORK

Sir Roger and his wife Barbara had chosen the Cancer Research Campaign as the charity to benefit from the Lord Mayor's Appeal. Sadly, Barbara died from the disease in 1996 before she could see Sir Roger take office. At various functions during the mayoral year he was accompanied by one of his daughters.

Sir Roger was one of a small number of City men who have followed in the steps of their father to become Lord Mayor, Sir Kenneth Cork having been Lord Mayor in 1978.

Sir Roger qualified as a chartered accountant in 1969 and joined the family firm of Cork Gully which specialised in insolvency and corporate recovery work. He became a partner in 1971 and after a merger with Coopers & Lybrand (now part of PwC), he continued there as a partner. In 1994, Sir Roger Cork joined accountancy firm Moore Stephens as a senior partner to develop their corporate recovery practice, retiring in 1999.

As Lord Mayor, he undertook a charity bike ride in August 1997 cycling from John O'Groats to Lands End to support the Appeal. On his first day 'back at work' in September a lunch was organised as a celebration of his achievement at the Watermen's Hall for the several livery companies to which Sir Roger was connected.

Sir Roger Cork played his part in history by being the senior host on The Royal Yacht Britannia in both Karachi and Mumbai during one its final voyages. Business seminars, held on board in both locations, were rounded off with an evening reception and the Beating Retreat by the Royal Marines.

Sir Roger Cork died in 2002.

Mother livery company Bowyers (Master 1990-92).
Also: Master World Trader (1999-2000).

SIR RICHARD NICHOLS

Sir Richard has been involved with the City since birth, his father having been a long-serving Clerk of the Worshipful Company of Salters, and Sir Richard is a liveryman of the Salters' Company. He attended Christ's Hospital School, founded in London by King Edward VI who gave the School the use of the old Greyfriars Monastery buildings in Newgate Street. It admitted its first 380 children in November 1552 and the School band still takes part in the Lord Mayor's Show.

Having qualified as a solicitor, Sir Richard spent time in Hong Kong. Following his return to England, he became a partner in a Watford law practice, retiring in 2002. He and his wife, Shelagh, also enjoyed farming in Hertfordshire. The mayoral year spent at the Mansion House therefore represented a significant change of lifestyle from rural to urban life.

His mayoral theme was 'International City - Serving the World'. During his overseas visits, Sir Richard was impressed by the high regard for the UK's higher education sector and believed it could be an ambassador for the financial services of the UK and City of London. Accordingly, he founded the Mansion House Scholarship Scheme. The Scheme, which continues to thrive, has been established as a grant-giving charity. It is designed to make scholarships available to overseas students taking Master's-level degree courses at British universities or for training in the financial services industry. The principal source of funding continues to be the livery companies. To date, more than 120 students from 50 countries have benefitted.

Mother livery company Salters (Master 1988-89).

Peter Edwards

1998

Oil on canvas

125 x 100cms (50 x 40ins)

Salters' Hall

Photograph of painting:
Michael Chevis

THE LORD LEVENE OF PORTSOKEN KBE

The Mayoral Appeal of Lord Levene was directed towards the building of a new leukaemia treatment centre at Hammersmith Hospital. To raise significant funding, Lord Levene at the start of his mayoralty persuaded the Department of Health to match charitable funding, an agreement he announced at his Lord Mayor's Banquet.

From 1985 to 1991, Lord Levene advised the British Government on achieving better value for money and served as a Permanent Secretary in the Ministry of Defence as Chief of Defence Procurement 1985-1991. Returning to the private sector, he became Deputy Chairman at Wasserstein Perella and, subsequently, Chairman of Bankers Trust International. In 1992 he was appointed by the Prime Minister as his Adviser on Efficiency and Effectiveness. He had also taken on the post of Chairman of the Docklands Light Railway and, subsequently, the chairmanship of the Canary Wharf development. He was elected as Chairman of Lloyd's of London in 2002, a post which he retained until 2011.

During his mayoralty, a new Guildhall Art Gallery was opened by Her Majesty the Queen and this enabled the public to be able to view, in a magnificent new location, the Corporation of London's unique art collection, the display of which had been limited by the old gallery's damage by fire during the Second World War.

Lord Levene visited more than 30 countries during his mayoralty and one of his visits was to Lebanon during which he was driven in a bulletproof car to meet Walid Jumblatt, the Druze leader, who lived in his own fortified enclave high above the city of Beirut.

In early November 1999, just before the end of his mayoralty, Lord Levene hosted a luncheon to mark the end of the 20th century at the Mansion House which was called 'A Celebration of Achievement', graced by the Queen as guest of honour. Achievers from all walks of life were invited, among whom was 90-year-old Abraham 'Abe' Beame, the only English-born Mayor of New York City. Seating protocols were abandoned, allowing for a fascinating juxtaposition of high achievers from every walk of life.

Mother livery company Carmen (Master 1992-93).

Andrew Festing

1999

Oil on canvas

100 x 75cms (40 x 30ins)

City of London School

Reproduced by permission of the John Carpenter Club

SIR CLIVE MARTIN OBE TD DL

For his Lord Mayor's Appeal Sir Clive chose Barnardo's, with which he has had a long involvement, and was delighted that the Appeal raised significant funds. A Sheep Drive across London Bridge was arranged and not only raised a considerable sum for the charity but also demonstrated to participants how difficult it is to walk a sheep on a lead!*

Sir Clive's career has been in the printing and publishing trade. After joining the family firm of Staples Printers in 1961, he became group managing director in 1972 and chairman in 1978. Having served in the armed forces continuously for more than sixty years, he has held various appointments in the Royal Engineers and the Honourable Artillery Company and commanded the Guard of Honour at St Paul's Cathedral for Her Majesty the Queen's Silver Jubilee Service.

The mayoral year of 1999-2000 included Millennium Eve celebrations at North Greenwich. Sir Clive accompanied Prime Minister Tony Blair and the Leader of the Opposition by underground train to the opening of the Millennium Dome Experience on New Year's Eve 1999.

A keen walker, Sir Clive was delighted that his mayoralty coincided with the opening of the Millennium Footbridge linking the City with Bankside, adjacent to Tate Modern. The bridge was almost immediately closed as oscillation occurred from a tendency of people to synchronise their walking rhythm. With damping devices installed, the bridge reopened. Sir Clive was a great advocate of the City looking outward and the concept of the Millennium Footbridge reflected this thinking and aligned with his mayoral theme for the year of 'The Creative City'.

To promote British financial services, Sir Clive visited many countries, in particular those applying for accession in 2004 to the European Union. As Alderman for Aldgate Ward he was particularly keen to support UK maritime interests as this is the City area from where much of this business sector operates.

Mother livery company Stationers and Newspaper Makers (Master 1997-98).
Also: Master Chartered Secretaries and Administrators (2004-05); Master of Guild of Freemen of the City of London (1995-96).

*The medieval right to take sheep across London Bridge without paying a toll was a privilege of Freemen of the City of London. Sheep drives have become a more frequent charitable event.

David Cobley

2000

Oil on canvas

152 x 122cms (60 x 48ins)

Stationers' Hall

"I first met Sir Clive coming down the stairs at Mansion House and immediately thought it would be a good setting. I didn't want the grandeur of the place to overshadow the man - I wanted his personality to shine through. The setting actually incorporates elements from two different staircases within the building."
DAVID COBLEY

SIR DAVID HOWARD Bt

Sir David's father and grandfather each served as Lord Mayor, making the family the first to have three successive generations elected to the mayoralty. Sir David is the 3rd Baronet Howard of Great Rissington, and inherited the baronetcy from his father in 2001. In his grandfather's day the Lord Mayor was usually created a baronet as was the case with Sir Seymour Howard.

The theme of Sir David's mayoralty was 'Marketplace of the World', reflecting the importance to the country of international business and income from the financial, shipping and commodities markets operating in the City of London. His own business career has been spent in the City stockbroking company, Charles Stanley. Sir David has been managing director since 1988 and chairman since 1999, growing the firm into one of the largest retail stockbrokers in the UK.

His Lord Mayor's Appeal raised a substantial sum towards a new women's cancer centre of excellence at St Bartholomew's Hospital in the City.

Speaking at his Lord Mayor's Banquet, Sir David raised the question of the stalled Crossrail project being re-launched, earlier proposals apparently having been abandoned. Prime Minister Tony Blair responded to the Lord Mayor's speech, acknowledging the importance of the project to Greater London and offered his government's backing. Construction is proceeding and rail services are scheduled to commence in 2018.

Sir David visited South America including Argentina at a time of improving relations between the two countries and increasing exports from the UK. He also visited Uruguay, the first visit for many years to that country by a Lord Mayor.

Mother livery company Gardeners (Master 1990-91).

Nicola J (Nicky) Philipps

2001

Oil on canvas

152 x 127cms (60 x 50ins)

Offices of Charles Stanley

SIR MICHAEL OLIVER DL

For the Lord Mayor's Show in 2001, the Lady Mayoress performed acrobatics under a helium balloon to promote 'The Square Smile', the name given to the Appeal for the year. The Appeal supported five mental health projects and two homeless charities and Sir Michael focused his efforts on mental health services for young people who, in particular, he felt need help to overcome very challenging problems.

In 1970, on returning to England from South Africa, Sir Michael joined City stockbrokers Kitcat & Aitken and his career gradually moved into investment management. He became director of investment funds following the merger of Scottish Widows with Lloyds Investment Managers.

During the 1960s, Sir Michael ran a paper-coating factory in Cape Town. Back in England, he joined, in 1970, a group of enthusiasts who carried out the first Thames-side warehouse apartment conversion in Wapping. The magnificent tea warehouse at Oliver's Wharf had been built by Sir Michael's great-great-grandfather on the site of the family's ironworks that had once supplied cannon and iron items for merchant ships.

Sir Michael's mayoralty coincided with Her Majesty the Queen's Golden Jubilee. A Service of Thanksgiving at St Paul's Cathedral was followed by a Guildhall luncheon for the Queen hosted by Sir Michael.

On its way to St Paul's, the Royal Procession paused at Temple Bar for the Ceremony of the Sword. This ancient ceremony takes place at the boundary between Westminster and the City and the site is today marked by a monument unveiled in 1880 to replace Sir Christopher Wren's Temple Bar gateway.

In accordance with tradition, and as depicted in the portrait, the Lord Mayor offered the City's Pearl Sword, so called because of the decoration of its sheath, to the Queen as an act of fidelity. The Monarch does not ask to be admitted to the City, although a contrary view has often been expressed.

The Lord Mayor's overseas visits included his key message that the relaxation of trade barriers would help to alleviate poverty. This heartfelt message reflected Sir Michael's long association with two charities providing accommodation for the homeless.

Mother livery company Ironmongers (Master 1991-92).

Alexander Talbot Rice

2005

Oil on canvas

127 x 152cms (50 x 60ins)

Ironmongers' Hall

This unusual portrait recreates the Ceremony (mentioned alongside) when the Lord Mayor welcomes Her Majesty the Queen to the City with the Ceremony of the Sword. "I was delighted to have the honour of painting the Queen, who agreed to leave the warmth of Buckingham Palace to sit in the Gold State Coach in the draughty Royal Mews for three separate sittings. The Queen was very kind to me and this portrait unusually illustrates HM with a very animated smile."
ALEXANDER TALBOT RICE

SIR GAVYN ARTHUR

Sir Gavyn was the first practising barrister to serve as Lord Mayor and his mayoralty was characterised by his promotion of the City as an international centre for commercial arbitration. He believes the English legal framework is superior to European and other codified legal frameworks that exist, a view he espoused while delivering the annual Denning Lecture entitled 'The City and the Law' in September 2003. He laid a particular emphasis on the legal profession in London continuing to act to maintain London's pre-eminence in the global legal system. This pre-eminence remains an important component in attracting business to London and the City in particular.

As a barrister, Sir Gavyn specialised in family finance law and in 1987 he chaired the Research Committee on Child Care Proceedings. Sir Gavyn was appointed a Deputy High Court Judge in 2008.

His Lord Mayor's Appeal supported Save the Children with the dual aim of raising awareness of problems faced by children in deprived areas of London.

His mayoral year saw him visiting 27 countries as well as hosting a very successful Guildhall banquet to receive President Putin of Russia. This took place during the first state visit by a Russian leader to Britain since Tsar Alexander II in 1874. He was also host to a left-of-centre conference for heads of state which included Prime Minister Tony Blair and former US president Bill Clinton.

When Rowan Williams was installed as Archbishop of Canterbury, it was Sir Gavyn's privilege to welcome him to the City with luncheon at the Mansion House.

Sir Gavyn resigned from the Court of Aldermen following his appointment in 2007 as a Circuit Judge, followed by the appointment as Deputy High Court Judge in 2008.

Mother livery company Gardeners (Master 2007-08).
Also: Master Wax Chandler (2012-2013);
Master Public Relations Practitioner (2010-11)
(a company without livery);
Master of Guild of Freemen of the City of London
(2009-10).

Valerie Wiffen

2003

Oil on linen

132 x 70cms (52 x 27.5ins)

Guildhall Art Gallery

SIR ROBERT FINCH DL

Sir Robert's mayoralty coincided with the centenary of the founding of the London Symphony Orchestra (LSO). His Lord Mayor's Appeal, 'Music and the Arts for Everyone', was very successful in providing an endowment for the LSO's new music education centre, based at the former St Luke's Church. The church, dating from 1733, was probably designed by Nicholas Hawksmoor and John James and was intended to provide for the increasing population in the areas around the City. Maintenance programmes during the 19th and 20th centuries were undone by subsidence, resulting in the church being abandoned until the 1990s. The vision of the LSO, also supported with funding from UBS, enabled the rebuilding of the church. During his year of office, Sir Robert's Appeal arranged concerts at the Barbican performed by the LSO in the presence of Her Majesty the Queen, at Canary Wharf and at Windsor Castle. The orchestra also performed at the Mansion House on the occasion of a Viennese Ball supporting the Appeal.

After qualifying as a solicitor in 1969, Sir Robert joined Linklaters international law practice. He became a partner in 1974 and, in 1996, joined the firm's management board to become head of the commercial property division. In 2005, he retired from Linklaters on being appointed as chairman of Liberty International plc.

In May 2004, the European Union was substantially enlarged with several Eastern European and Baltic states and Malta and Cyprus joining as new members. As Lord Mayor, Sir Robert hosted a dinner for the new EU members and the opportunity was taken to arrange bilateral meetings with UK government officials. He travelled to the new member states to promote the City's range of financial services and its skills and knowledge of international markets as well as a wide range of trips further afield.

Sir Robert's mayoralty included some unusual sea voyages. He journeyed by launch from Helsinki to Tallinn in very rough seas and gale-force winds and on another occasion, after fog grounded his flight, he again took to a launch to cross the Channel from Guernsey for a meeting in South West England.

Mother livery company Solicitors (Master 2000-01).
Also: Master Innholder (2009-10).

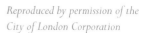

SIR MICHAEL SAVORY

Sir Michael's mayoral theme was 'Promoting Excellence' and he focused actively on promoting the international business expertise of the City of London and UK financial services generally.

Sir Michael's business career was in stockbroking and in 1967 he joined Foster and Braithwaite. When the business was sold in 1987, he joined Midland Bank where he was responsible for developing products for retail stock market investors. Following the merger with HSBC, Sir Michael was appointed a director and then chairman of the stockbroking division of HSBC.

He believed that the maritime industry was not recognised for its importance to the UK economy as insurers, shippers and brokers all tended to act separately. It became one of his priorities as Lord Mayor, therefore, to promote this sector and support the Chamber of Shipping. He visited major world ports including Hamburg, a former Hanseatic port with strong links formed during 600 years of trading with the City of London. Beside the Thames, the Steelyard was a walled area where Hanseatic merchants were based on the site of what is now Cannon Street Station.

There was also a wider maritime theme to Sir Michael's mayoralty. October 2005 was the 200th anniversary of the Battle of Trafalgar and he was involved in planning a re-enactment of the funeral of Lord Nelson with a large flotilla which sailed upstream from Greenwich to the City. A replica of a traditional shallop, Jubilant - a small rowboat built for the Her Majesty the Queen's Golden Jubilee - acted as a funeral barge and carried a copy of the New Trafalgar Dispatch to the Dean of St Paul's Cathedral, where Nelson is buried. The Dispatch was a modern version of Vice Admiral Collingwood's report on the Battle which brought the bittersweet news of the historic victory and the sad death of Lord Nelson, modified to include additional references to the courage and sacrifice of the sailors.

Sir Michael arranged an annual commemorative service to the achievements of Admiral Phillip, the first Governor of New South Wales, Australia, held at the City church of St Mary-le-Bow. He has been chairman of the Arthur Philip Memorial Trust since 1996.

Mother livery company Poulters (Master 1996-97).
Also: Master Clockmaker (1998-99).

Edward Goodridge

2004

Oil on canvas

81 x 66cms (32 x 26ins)

Guildhall Art Gallery

Reproduced by permission of the City of London Corporation

SIR DAVID BREWER CMG CVO

Sir David was educated at St Paul's School and the University of Grenoble, going on to pursue an international career in insurance broking. He gained extensive experience in Asia which proved invaluable for his mayoralty and the City generally. He opened his firm's Tokyo office, living there for three years, followed by establishing their office in China in 1981 and subsequently their representative office in Mumbai.

Sir David is recognised for building the City's relationship with China, an important legacy. In 2007 he became chairman of the China-Britain Business Council (CBBC), the leading British organisation promoting trade and investment between the UK and China. He has continued to push forward CBBC's contribution to UK-China trade and business exchange, making well over 100 trips to China.

Sir David hails from Cornwall and, in a wonderful example of 'the City coming to the country', he arranged during his mayoralty for the Honourable Artillery Company (HAC) to attend the Royal Cornwall Show in June 2006. The Company of Pikemen and Musketeers of the HAC provides the personal bodyguard to the Lord Mayor and Lady Mayoress and so it was very appropriate that The Light Cavalry Unit escorted the Lady Mayoress on to the showground, thereby re-creating the atmosphere of the Lord Mayor's Show. They were accompanied by members of over eighty livery companies and the whole spectacle was much enjoyed by visitors. He was President of the London Cornish Association from 2005 to 2013. His mayoralty is greatly remembered for the warm personality of himself and his wife, Tessa.

Sir David chose the Treloar Trust as the beneficiary of his Lord Mayor's Appeal for the year which coincided with the launch of Treloar's Centenary Appeal. The Appeal aimed to provide modernised facilities at both the School and the College together with a pilot project to assist students to progress on to independent life. For the Lord Mayor's Show, the Treloar Trust float featured a giant revolving birthday cake celebrating 100 years of success in supporting young people with physical disabilities.

Sir David Brewer was appointed Lord-Lieutenant of Greater London by Her Majesty the Queen in April 2008.

Mother livery company Merchant Taylors (Master 2001-02).

June Mendoza

2006

Oil on canvas

127 x 107cms (50 x 42ins)

Merchant Taylors' Hall

Reproduced with the kind permission of the Merchant Taylors' Company

SIR JOHN STUTTARD

For his mayoralty, Sir John focused on two connected themes: a business theme of 'City of London, City of Learning' and the Lord Mayor's Appeal theme, 'Sharing Skills, Changing Lives'. He is passionate about education and has been since his own experience of working for Voluntary Service Overseas. During his many overseas visits as Lord Mayor, Sir John emphasised the availability in London of high quality business education and training opportunities.

After qualifying as a chartered accountant, he was made a partner in Coopers & Lybrand in 1975. From 1981 to 1983 he was seconded to the Cabinet Office, advising on privatisation and restructuring of nationalised industries. In 1994, he began a very successful five-year appointment as executive chairman of Coopers & Lybrand, China. On his return to the UK, Sir John became a senior client partner in the merged firm of PricewaterhouseCoopers, retaining links with business in China.

As Lord Mayor, Sir John felt a particular affinity with Richard Whittington who was Alderman of the same City ward, Lime Street, exactly 600 years earlier, in 1406. Whittington, Lord Mayor of the City four times (today only one term is served), was extremely generous and left his fortune to charities connected with the City. The charities continue today to assist people in need. Folklore stories of Dick Whittington seeking his fortune in London were first recorded in the 17th century from which plays and pantomimes have developed. In reality, Richard Whittington was a very successful wool and cloth merchant and a liveryman of the Mercers' Company.

Highlights of the mayoral year included Her Majesty the Queen's official City visits to celebrate the 25th anniversary of the opening of the Barbican Centre and the Centenary of the opening of the Central Criminal Court building (better known as the Old Bailey) which is managed and funded by the City of London.

Sir John Stuttard became the sponsoring Alderman of the Guild of Educators in 2001, assisting them to achieve full livery status in September 2013 as the 109th livery company in the City of London. During this year he became Master of the Company.

Mother livery company Glaziers & Painters of Glass (Master 2009-10).
Also: Master Educator (2013-14) and Master Chartered Accountant (2011-12).

Petri Anderson

2007

Stained Glass

102 x 81cms (40 x 32ins)

Glaziers' Hall

"*The portrait was a commission that I relished. I've done portraits before and it is always exciting; it takes some work to really bring the likeness through in this medium. The challenge is to present the man of today, his achievement and position while stylistically linking back through the history of the mayoralty. Referencing medieval portraiture the portrait includes the arms of the Lord Mayor and of the Glaziers' Company and is set in Mansion House.*"
PETRI ANDERSON

SIR DAVID LEWIS DL

Sir David's Lord Mayor's Appeal supported two charities very close to his and his wife's hearts: Orbis International, for which funds raised were used to build two eye clinics in India, and Wellbeing of Women, which was undertaking a major miscarriage research project.

In 1969, Sir David joined City solicitors Norton Rose and was elected a partner in 1976. He relocated to Hong Kong for three years, serving as global head of corporate finance. From 1997 to 2003 he was senior partner and chairman of Norton Rose.

At the end of a typically busy day as Lord Mayor, Sir David reflected on his role and recorded thoughts along these lines: "…there are only 165 days before I pass the baton to the next Lord Mayor who has not the faintest idea of the stress and the enjoyment awaiting him. I decide that public service is fine but there cannot be many jobs where you have to take two years off paid employment, work so hard unpaid with no expenses and end up poorer. But then I cannot think of a job where you have so much variety, meet such interesting people, travel so much globally, live in such a lovely house, can speak your own mind, cannot be fired and where, on your own territory, you are second only to the Sovereign."

This was after a banquet at Guildhall on the occasion of a state visit by President Sarkozy of France accompanied by his wife, Carla Bruni. Indeed, this particular day had started earlier than most with a dawn visit to Smithfield meat market. Coming from a Carmarthenshire sheep community, Sir David was very interested in the market sales to the hotel and restaurant trade.

His mayoralty coincided with the 2008 global financial crisis and Sir David was steadfast in his support of the City of London in his many overseas visits which were well informed by his own international business experience.

Mother livery company Solicitors (Master 2009-10).

IAN LUDER CBE

Ian was the first Londoner for several years to become Lord Mayor. He was born in Mile End and several past Lord Mayors have had connections with the East End. In the late 13th century, Mayor* Henry le Waleys, who owned a mansion in Stepney, negotiated with King Edward I to have City liberties confirmed. He also established a market for the sale of fish and meat on what is now the site of the Mansion House. Rents were used for the upkeep of London Bridge. Henry Colet, also owning property in Stepney, was a wealthy mercer and Lord Mayor in the 15th century. His son, John Colet, founded St Paul's School, initially located in the City, but, since 1968, sited in Barnes, south west London.

Ian is a chartered accountant and tax specialist. Articled to Arthur Andersen, he left after qualifying to become a partner in MacIntyre Hudson, returning to Andersen's in 1988 as a partner. He left in 2002 when he was appointed a partner in Grant Thornton, remaining there until 2009.

His Mayoral Appeal supported, firstly, St John Ambulance and the provision of defibrillators in all public City buildings. The equipment could be used without training and could detect that the person taken ill had suffered coronary arrest. Secondly, he supported The Lord's Taverners, which funds facilities for deprived and physically disadvantaged young people.

The mayoral year of 2008-09 was a period of economic uncertainty following the banking failures of 2007 and 2008. Ian was consistent in his messages that financial services are crucial to the long-term success of the UK economy with the need to maintain an ethical approach to business. It was fitting, therefore, that his mayoral theme was 'Building Financial Literacy for the Nation'.

Ian is a Past Master of the Company of Tax Advisers. Having been its sponsoring Alderman, Ian is the first Master of the Company of Arts Scholars since attaining their livery status in February 2014.

Mother livery company Coopers.
Also: Master Tax Adviser (1999-2001) and Master Art Scholar (2014-15).

*The title 'Lord Mayor' is purely customary, but of great age. In the thirteenth century the Latin 'dominus major' is found and, in 1414, the English 'Lord Mair'.

Sophie Gilbart Denham

2010

Oil on canvas

122 x 102cms (48 x 40ins)

Coopers' Hall

"The request was for a portrait in full ceremonial dress. I was very aware to not let the detail take over the portrait and to achieve a balance between the history and the man. Generally I prefer to use bolder brush strokes but on this occasion I had to get more intricate. I had the sitter holding his gloves to add a touch of informality."
SOPHIE GILBART DENHAM

NICK ANSTEE

The Lord Mayor's Appeal, 'Pitch Perfect', combined two elements. His objective was to assist children from deprived areas to have access to musical and cricketing opportunities to play and perform in teams and groups. Chance to Shine, formed in 2005 to improve access to competitive sport for state school pupils, has continued to reverse the decline in schools' cricket. Over two million participants have benefited from this initiative which, during Nick's mayoralty, included a game being played on the concourse of Waterloo Station.

Nick qualified as a chartered accountant in 1982 and joined the global law firm King & Wood Mallesons in 2007, bringing with him the experience of having previously been lead partner of Andersen's private equity advisory practice, before transferring to Deloitte in 2002. As a corporate finance adviser, Nick has worked on a number of complex cross-border transactions. He was awarded an honorary corporate finance qualification by the ICAEW Corporate Finance Faculty in recognition of his "distinct and significant contribution to the corporate finance industry".

Nick Anstee brought an unusually high level of sporting achievement to the mayoralty as he ran his 17th London Marathon during the year. As part of his training for the event, he completed the New York Marathon a week before he assumed office and managed to fit in a half-marathon while on an official visit to Bahrain.

His year of office was characterised by the continuing need to rebuild business confidence following the 2008 global financial crisis. He fully recognised this challenge, choosing as his mayoral theme 'Forming the Future'. At the post-general election Mansion House annual Banquet for Bankers and Merchants, the new Chancellor of the Exchequer George Osborne outlined Coalition Government thinking on financial regulation. The Chancellor also noted that the City of London embodies entrepreneurial energy, innovation and a global outlook, all of which are needed for its success. The Chancellor's comments were very relevant to the ambassadorial role of the Lord Mayor, and Nick continued the work of the two previous Lord Mayors to promote the contribution made to the UK economic recovery by financial services.

Mother livery company Butchers (Master 2014-15).

Andrew Festing

2012

Oil on canvas

160 x 87cms (63 x 34ins)

Plaisterers' Hall

SIR MICHAEL BEAR

A distinctive flavour of Sir Michael's mayoralty was his business background in engineering and regeneration sectors, notably in leading the regeneration of Spitalfields. In that sense he represented the 'demand' side of the City's financial services as a client using such services. His year was focussed on outcomes, especially for overseas visits where he matched his delegations to opportunities in the market.

His mayoral theme was 'City of London, City of Choice'. It seemed appropriate, for example, that during his mayoral year a new cutting-edge design building was being completed for Rothschild Bank on the site that Rothschild's have occupied for 200 years alongside medieval St Swithin's Lane. The new building enhanced views from the lane of Wren's St Stephen Walbrook church, a transforming development that is characteristic of the City of London.

Sir Michael's career has been spent in the construction sector and more recently in property development. He became a member of the Institute of Civil Engineers in 1979, going on to be elected a Fellow of the Royal Institution of Chartered Surveyors and an Honorary Fellow of the Royal Academy of Engineering in 2010. Since 2009, Sir Michael has been a non-executive director of engineering consultancy Arup.

Sir Michael's Lord Mayor's Appeal was 'Bear Necessities - Building Better Lives' and supported the Thomas Coram Foundation, the UK's first children's charity which helps vulnerable children build their self-esteem and be able to make positive life choices. The Appeal also supported RedR which trains and provides engineers for worldwide disaster relief. A very successful Appeal event was a Georgian Ball held in the Mansion House. The Mansion House, sometimes described as a 'Georgian town palace', was completed in 1752 during the lifetime of the charity's founder, Thomas Coram.

Sir Michael has strong connections with Africa, having been born in Kenya and later having graduated from a South African university with an engineering degree. In recognition of these African origins, he was saluted at his Lord Mayor's Show outside the Mansion House by 18 Zulus. His daughter rode alongside the City Marshall in the Lord Mayor's Show procession.

Mother livery company Paviors (Master 2012-13).

Luke Martineau

2011

Oil on canvas

152 x 91cms (60 x 36ins)

Paviours' House

"I wanted to paint Sir Michael in a full length pose to allow true justice to be given to the robes and ceremonial attributes and I gave particular prominence to the sword. The painting is set in the Venetian Parlour at the Mansion House, the Lord Mayor's office and centre of his active life."
LUKE MARTINEAU

SIR DAVID WOOTTON

The theme of Sir David's mayoralty was to reconnect the City with the rest of the UK. To this end, he displayed in the Mansion House examples of Stoke on Trent pottery and mannequins showing examples of Yorkshire woollen clothing reflecting his northern roots. The trauma unit at Royal London Hospital was the major beneficiary of his Lord Mayor's Appeal. He also supported two rowing charities and a playing fields charity.

Even as Lord Mayor, Sir David was able to indulge his passion for rowing. During overseas mayoral visits, he grasped opportunities with the Grasshopper Rowing Club in Zurich to row in a 24-scull boat and at the Tigre Rowing Club in Buenos Aires he rowed with Argentine Olympic team members. Rio saw him rowing in a coxless four over the 2016 Olympic rowing course. For the Lord Mayor's Show, he reintroduced a river pageant which harked back to Shows up until the mid-19th century when the new Lord Mayor would travel by row barge to Westminster to swear the Oath of Allegiance to the Monarch. The new river pageant travels downstream with the Lord Mayor disembarking near the Tower of London before making their way to Guildhall to start the Procession in the State Coach.

Sir David qualified as a solicitor with Allen & Overy in 1975. He was admitted to the partnership in 1979 and was the longest serving partner in the firm, leading on major client engagements in the field of corporate finance until his retirement in March 2015.

A high point of Sir David's mayoral year was Her Majesty the Queen's Diamond Jubilee celebrations in June 2012 and the Service of Thanksgiving at St Paul's Cathedral. He enjoyed interacting with the Mayor of London, Boris Johnson, who commissioned a Greek Ode for the 2012 London Olympic Games. This was installed in the Olympic Park and during Opening Ceremony celebrations was recited by Boris at the Royal Opera House. Sir David was delighted to present medals at the 2012 Paralympic Games.

Mother livery company Fletchers (Master 2005-06).
Also: Master Solicitor (2010-11).

Jane Bond

2012

Oil on canvas

112 x 99cms (44 x 39ins)

In private ownership

SIR ROGER GIFFORD

A strong arts theme ran through Sir Roger's mayoralty, amplifying the City's strong role in this area. Comprehensive guidebooks to the Harold Samuel Collection of paintings and statues in the Mansion House were produced by Clare, Lady Gifford, and many concerts were held in the Mansion House throughout the year. Sir Roger's favourite painting from the collection by Gerard ter Borch is evidenced in his portrait.

Central to this focus was the magnificent organ presented to Her Majesty the Queen by the Lord Mayor and the City in celebration of her Diamond Jubilee. The organ lived in the Egyptian Hall before being moved to its permanent home in the Lady Chapel at Westminster Abbey. The Lord Mayor played his recorder, also seen in the portrait, at a Musicians' Company banquet.

The Lord Mayor's Appeal funded the setting up of a charity, the City Music Foundation, supporting young musicians. In its first two years, 17 musicians and groups benefited from the programme.

His business themes focussed on the City as an international financial centre for the whole of Europe, as well as its role as a global centre for philanthropy, including asset management and charity and trust law.

Sir Roger's career has been in banking, initially with SG Warburg and then with Skandinaviska Enskilda Bank (SEB), where he worked in equity and debt capital markets. After six years in Japan, he returned to London and is head of SEB in the UK.

Sir Roger's mother livery company is the Musicians and he is also a Cordwainer, evidenced by the shoebox in the portrait. He is a member of the International Bankers, the Security Professionals and the Guild of Public Relations Practitioners. Readers may form their own view as to which of these the gentleman in the ter Borch painting represents.

As a Scot, Sir Roger provided whisky and Scottish 'tablet' at all the Mansion House dinners. It therefore seemed only fitting that he arranged for the Lady Mayoress's 51st birthday to be celebrated with an evening entitled 'The Reel of the 51st'. The Egyptian Hall was swathed in tartan and some 250 guests danced into the night.

Mother livery company Musicians.
Also: Master International Banker (2011).

Andre de Moller

2014

Oil on canvas

76 x 66cms (30 x 26ins)

Cordwainers' Offices

"I wanted to paint 'the man' and so we didn't use the ceremonial robes. However, I did want to create a classical composition and so, inspired by the seventeenth century Dutch paintings in the Mansion House, we included instead items such as his favourite painting from the collection, his father's old watch, which he wears constantly, a recorder which he plays, a shoebox representing the Cordwainers and a map of the world implying he is well travelled."
ANDRE DE MOLLER

Photograph of painting:
Gerald Sharp Photography

DAME FIONA WOOLF CBE

Dame Fiona is an energy lawyer with a global legal practice and has worked in over 40 jurisdictions. She was the second female president of The Law Society of England and Wales in 2006-07.

As Lord Mayor she issued her '686 Plan' which set out her programme covering The Lord Mayor's Appeal, The Power of Diversity, The Lord Mayor's Charity Leadership Programme and Tomorrow's City, all under her mayoral theme - 'The Energy to Transform Lives'. Her Appeal supported four community-based charities - Beating Bowel Cancer, Princess Alice Hospice, Raleigh International and Working Chance - and was placed on a permanent footing (rather than being set up afresh each year) using the recently incorporated charitable company, The Lord Mayor's Appeal. This captures the efficiencies and communications necessary in the electronic age but still achieves an annual freshness and a platform for promoting philanthropy; it has also been an effective vehicle to promote diversity and inclusion.

Among highlights of the Appeal programme was the abseil event down the Lloyd's of London building, undertaken by many leading women in the City, including the Lord Mayor herself, Lloyd's Chief Executive and the first female Master Mercer. The Lord Mayor's Opera unsurprisingly took 'Powerful Women' as its theme. Her 686 logo, designed by Grant MacDonald, is shown at the foot of the page.

The Power of Diversity programme, promoted on three London buses sponsored by 34 City firms, was a major theme to help put diversity firmly on the City map. The participants asked the City Corporation to continue the programme after the end of Dame Fiona's mayoralty.

Tomorrow's City developed thought leadership in the long term, focusing on the future regulation of financial services, financing and implementing long-term infrastructure and how cities will develop in the future. All of these were constant subjects on her mayoral visits abroad.

The Charity Leadership Programme, chaired by her husband, Nicholas, was focused on the skills and tools that chairmen need in order to lead more effective boards. It was also successful in attracting potential chairmen of charities to volunteer. The programme was actively supported by the Cass Business School, Mazars and Macquarie.

Mother livery company Solicitors (Master 2015-16).

Richard Stone

2014

Oil on canvas

122 x 91cms (48 x 36ins)

Wax Chandlers' Hall

"I was delighted to paint the portrait of Dame Fiona. With her charm and elegance I decided to paint her wearing her official hat, an unusual choice, as I felt she looked marvellous in it. Another unusual step was to include the scarlet robe because Fiona was able to carry it off with grace and presence."
RICHARD STONE

THE ARTISTS